Made in United States
Orlando, FL
03 May 2022

17448984R00074